Colonel Stephens' Railmotors

By
Stephen Garrett
and
John Scott-Morgan

The second Ford set on the Kent & East Sussex waits in brand new splendour in the loop platform at Tenterden Town in 1924. Photograph Colonel Stephens Railway Museum.

Copyright Irwell Press 1995
ISBN 1-871608-46-5
Printed by The Amadeus Press, Huddersfield
Irwell Press,
P.O.Box 1260,
Caernarfon,
Gwynedd, LL55 3ZD
Printed by The Amadeus Press, Huddersfield

IRWELL
PRESS ⩶

Contents

FOREWORD

Holman Fred Stephens, born on 15th November 1868, was best known as the manager and engineer to various independent standard and narrow gauge railways. Some of these railways had been associated with Stephens from the planning stage whilst others sought out his services when his reputation for running railways on a shoestring began to spread. He was also associated with the engineering and construction of a number of other railways on which he held no subsequent management role, and with the planning and promotion of a number of railways for which authority was refused or which failed to attract sufficient investment for them to be built.

The railways associated with Stephens were quite separate concerns but had many features in common. Most were built under the Light Railways Act 1896 or subsequently brought within the provisions of that Act, which allowed railways to be built and operated to less exacting standards than those to be found on the main lines. Stephens' railways were therefore cheaply built and cheaply run. Frequently this was achieved by the purchase of second-hand equipment and his railways became famous as living museums of rolling stock, signalling and track discarded by the larger railway companies.

Stephens was, however, not an antiquarian. He was an early member of the Royal Flying Club and an enthusiastic motorist. He was quite happy to seek out and employ new ideas on his railways if they offered economies in operation without too much capital outlay. His railways were early pioneers in the use of concrete for the construction of bridges and sleepers but it was his early use of internal combustion vehicles for which he is perhaps best remembered as an innovator.

Stephens' first connection with this form of propulsion seems to have been his proposal of a Hornsby-Ackroyd compression ignited oil locomotive for operating services on the narrow gauge Rye & Camber Tramway. The Tramway had opened in 1895 but the Directors seem to have been happier to go for the known qualities of steam locomotion than to experiment with internal combustion. Stephens eventually obtained a small petrol locomotive for the Tramway in 1925 and also experimented, with varying degrees of success, with a selection of internal combustion shunters on the Festiniog and Welsh Highland Railways. Apart from two adapted Fordson tractors on the Weston Clevedon & Portishead Railway, Stephens does not appear to have tried to acquire petrol or diesel locomotives for his standard gauge railways but did make extensive use of petrol railmotors* on them. These and the steam railmotors which preceded them are the subject of this book.

*The description 'railmotor' was just one of the terms used to describe self-propelled passenger vehicles but was the term most frequently used until the 1930s. Other terms included 'rail motor cars', 'rail motor omnibuses', 'petrol motor vehicles' and 'petrol rail cars'. To avoid confusion we have stuck to 'railmotor'.

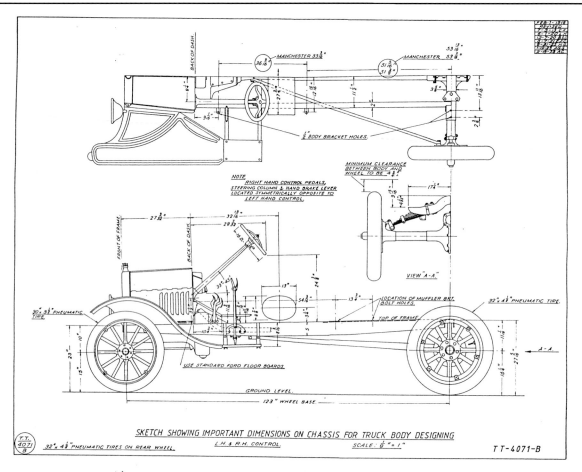

The raw materials: Ford drawing of their truck chassis found amongst the records of the Festiniog Railway and dated 1923. Photograph Festiniog Railway Archives.

Railmotor design found amongst the papers of the Festiniog Railway. Unfortunately not reproduced to scale, it appears to show a standard gauge proposal, rather than one specifically for the Festiniog. Photograph Festiniog Railway Archives.

Chapter One
THE STEAM RAILMOTOR

Holman Stephens' first example of a self-propelled passenger carrying vehicle was a steam railmotor purchased in 1905 for the Kent & East Sussex Railway. Steam tramcars had seen some success in the 19th Century but it was not until 1902 that a major British railway, the London & South Western, had taken up the idea of steam railmotors. The idea was rapidly gathered up by other railway companies and manufacturers and it is a clear sign of Stephens' innovative approach to railway operation that he entered this field at such an early date.

Stephens' interest in steam railmotors may have been due to the introduction of such a machine on the Sheppey Light Railway, by the South Eastern & Chatham Railway in 1904. Stephens had been the engineer to the independent company which had promoted and constructed this line and he would have had a considerable knowledge of its

operation. Stephens' railmotor was, however, a very different sort of design from that running on the Sheppey Light or anywhere else.

The steam railmotors of this period were typically bogie vehicles with either a steam-powered bogie or an articulated engine unit. The locomotive section might be fully enclosed within the carriage body or protrude from its end, giving the impression of a diminutive locomotive that had reversed rather smartly into the carriagework. There were enormous variations in designs and the power units might be four-coupled, six-coupled or single driven.

Stephens' railmotor differed from the normal designs not only in having just four wheels but in its form of transmission. Instead of adopting a scaled down version of conventional locomotive cylinders and valve gear it was fitted with a pair of vertical cylinders driving a layshaft which drove the front axle,

geared down 2.25 to 1, by means of a roller chain. The following dimensions for this vehicle are given in the *Kent & East Sussex Rolling Stock Register* and differ in some respects from dimensions quoted by other sources:

Steam Rail Motor No.6
Built by Messrs R & Y Pickering & Co Ltd, Wishaw, N.B. 1905
Delivered to K & E.S.Railway Coy 3/05
Length over buffers 30ft. 0 in.
Width over Body 9ft. 0in.
Length over Body 27ft. 1in.
Height from Rail 10ft. 9in.
Diameter of Wheels 3ft. 0in.
Total Wheel Base 17ft. 0in.
Seating Accommodation 36 (Third Class only)
Engine & Boiler for above purchased from Messrs Hutchinson & Co 1904
Dia of Cylinders 5 in.

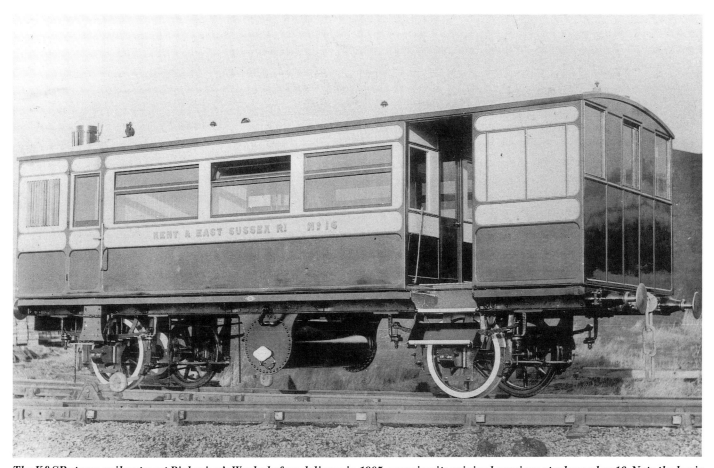

The K&SR steam railmotor at Pickering's Works before delivery in 1905, carrying its original carriage stock number 16. Note the basic suspension provided and the unpromising location of the water tank. Photograph John Scott Morgan Collection.

The steam railmotor at Rolvenden. Reputedly photographed in 1910 but possibly earlier. Note the waist panel repainted brown and the number 6 allocating it within the locomotive stock. The box fixture on the end is possibly an acetylene generator for lighting as a pipe runs from it up to the roof. Is the destination board purely decoration or has the railmotor really ventured out on the line?

R & Y Pickering were better known as carriage and wagon manufacturers and not only delivered three new carriages to the Kent & East Sussex Railway in May 1905 but had also converted six four wheeled carriages into three bogie carriages for the Railway in 1904. Since the firm was not otherwise known for designing or supplying motive power it seems quite likely that they constructed the railmotor either to Stephens' own design or at least to his specification. It is, however, possible that they had completed the vehicle for another purchaser but that the sale had fallen through and Stephens had acquired it instead. Pickering's own records do not appear to have survived and the Kent & East Sussex Archives have as yet revealed nothing on the question of the design of this vehicle.

The experience of the main line railway companies with steam railmotors was mixed. Some designs seem to have been hopeless from the start and no amount of remedial action could get them to perform satisfactorily. Others improved in time but required further design work and some, notably on the Great Western and on the Lancashire & Yorkshire, seem to have got it about right. Common problems were lack of power and adhesion and problems of discomfort arising from vibration and oscillation. Even those that worked satisfactorily posed problems of maintenance. Many of this generation of steam railmotors failed to survive the First World War.

Stephens' railmotor seems to have been doomed from the design stage. Its underframe and suspension would have been better suited to a carriage for the less demanding sort of passenger and made little allowance for the inevitable vibrations set up by the vertical cylinders. Moreover the vertical boiler was offset to one side of the vehicle which must have created problems of weight distribution. Water was carried in a cylindrical tank slung transversely beneath the centre point of the chassis. It is likely that some degree of surging took place within the tank and that this too would have affected the stability of the vehicle.

The Kent & East Sussex Rolling Stock Register records a steady series of major repairs to the railmotor from 1906 to 1913:

'New Crank Shaft made by Clarkes Crank & Forge Co Lincoln 1906 Engine thoroughly overhauled & repaired by S.E & C.Rly Coy at their marine works Dover 5/06. New Boiler purchased from Messrs White Bros, Stratford and put in 7/07. New Crank Shaft made by Clarkes Crank & Forge Coy Lincoln and put in 8/08. New Connecting rods made by J.Wright Tipton and put in Feb 1909. New set steel Tubes put in boiler Aug 1909. New Brass Eccentric Plummer Block Cap put on Aug 1909. Engine & Boiler overhauled March 1910. Engine & Boiler overhauled, Tubes new set May 1911. Engine and Boiler overhauled and fractured staunchions repaired June 1912. Body left side overhauled and renewed June 1913.'

A picture emerges of a vehicle trying to tear itself apart as it progressed along the line. Unfortunately we know of no photographs of the railmotor in service nor of any contemporary accounts of its service on the line. It must have been in use to have justified the repairs carried out and when an additional siding was put in at Bodiam in 1910 Stephens requested permission to erect a small platform alongside it so that the railmotor might pass other trains here. It is unfortunate that Ken Nunn, one of the few railway photographers to take an active interest in minor railways at this time, does not seem to have caught the railmotor in action during his visits to the Kent & East Sussex. It was probably under repair!

Photographs do survive of the railmotor at Pickering's works prior to delivery. These show that it was painted in the Railway's brown and ivory livery with a narrow ivory waist panel lettered KENT & EAST SUSSEX RY No 16, which indicates that it was originally intended to be included in the Railway's carriage stock. It was a straight sided vehicle like the carriages bought from Pickering later in 1905. At the powered end was an engine compartment entered by side doors. Above the waist panel on either side of the engine compartment were large vertically louvered panels hinged at the top, presumably for ventilation. The front of the engine compartment was divided into five vertical panels and painted in one dark colour, probably brown but possibly red, as Stephens had the brake ends of his Pickering carriages painted red. The upper sections of the outer and centre panels were glazed. Neither the end nor sides of the engine compartment had any apparent doorway or hatch large enough for removing the boiler for attention. Hook couplings with chains were provided at either end but were probably intended for towing the railmotor rather than for attaching wagons or other stock to be pulled by it.

Behind the engine compartment was a small smoking compartment which opened off a larger non smoking saloon. These two areas are alleged to have been capable of holding 31 passengers between them but it is not clear how this seating was arranged. The saloon opened into a transverse open passage. Beyond this was a further compartment intended for the driver or guard and for the accommodation of milk churns and up to ten passengers. This end of the railmotor was a mirror image of the other, with five vertical panels and three windows. The windows at each end were placed very much higher than the side windows.

A photograph believed to have been taken in 1910 shows the railmotor in running condition at Rolvenden. It shows certain differences from its appearance at Pickering's works. A destination board holder had been fitted above the central side window and held a board reading ROBERTSBRIDGE JCN when photographed. The waist panel had been painted brown and was now lettered K & E S R No 6. A lamp bracket had been fitted centrally on the non-powered end of the body. The photograph does not show the powered end but it is likely that this also carried a lamp bracket. Between the left hand and central end windows a curious cylindrical object had been fitted from which a thin pipe led to the roof. This may possibly have been an acetylene generator to provide lighting, although the usual style on the Kent & East Sussex was a large oblong box fitted on top of the roof.

As the Rolling Stock Register entries have shown, the left hand side of the railmotor had to be rebuilt in 1913. All subsequent photographs show considerable alterations to the ends of the railmotor as well but it is not known whether these were carried out at the same time as the alterations to the side. The repairs to the side seem to have been extensive but did not greatly alter the vehicle's appearance. The lower side panel and waist panel of the saloon area were divided into two panels instead of continuous panels as before and the upper panel to the non-powered end compartment was divided into two equal panels instead of the previous arrangement, of two narrow outer panels and two broader centre panels.

The alterations to the ends, whenever they were carried out, were substantial. At the non-powered end the windows in the outer and central panels were replaced by two windows reaching to waist level in the previously unglazed panels and the panels that had previously held windows were filled in. At the powered end a pair of doors that would not have looked out of place on a potting shed were inserted in front of the boiler, presumably for access, and a small top hinged window was fitted above the inner door. The original end windows in the other panels were replaced by panels down to waist level but a second small top-hinged window was fitted in the centre of what was originally an unglazed panel. The outside of the railmotor had then been painted brown all over but the transverse passage giving access to the saloon had been left in its original colours.

These alterations have been described in detail because they indicate a serious intention of continuing to operate the railmotor. There are, however, no more records of anyone seeing it in service after the First World War than before, and there are no further records of repairs in the Rolling Stock Register. The subsequent history of the railmotor is one of gradual decay in the yard at Rolvenden. Its overall coat of brown paint gradually weathered away and its original two tone paintwork reappeared. In 1932 Stephens' successor, W.H.Austen, applied to the Court of Chancery for permission to dispose of a number of surplus and worn out items of rolling stock. These included the railmotor: 'The steam rail car... has not been used for at least 15 years and is quite beyond repair. Its scrap value I estimate at the sum of £6.10.0..'

Even at this price no buyer seems to have been forthcoming and the railmotor continued to stand in Rolvenden yard. It appears to have remained substantially complete until 1935 when the double doors to the engine compartment disappeared and portions of the panelling and roof canvas began to lift. At some time after 1937 much of its plumbing appears to have been removed and almost the entire panel above the windows on the left side had come adrift.

The carcass of the railmotor actually survived most of the Railway's original locomotive fleet and even outlived the later petrol railmotors. It was finally broken up in 1943 so that its frame could provide the materials for the construction of a new water tower at Rolvenden. The water tower escaped the general destruction of the Rolvenden site by British Railways and is still standing today.

The railmotor in its decline. The shed doors have dropped off to reveal the vertical boiler in its off-set position. Considering that it had been out of use for twenty years or more the bodywork is still in fair condition.

Possibly the strangest locomotive operated by Holman Stephens was the diminutive tank engine GAZELLE. This had been built in 1893 by Alfred Dodman & Company of Kings Lynn for the private use of Mr William Burkitt, a prominent local businessman, who was able to persuade the main line companies to let him travel over their lines in it. It was a 2-2-2WT with seats for four passengers fitted where the coal bunker would normally be found. The footplate was without a cab or weatherboard and the passenger 'compartment' was also without any sort of roof, though it did have a small screen at the front which may have marginally reduced the numbers of cinders scorching its hardy occupants. Its dimensions were:

Driving wheels 3ft. 9in. diameter
Leading and trailing wheels 2ft. 3in. diameter
Wheelbase 10ft. 6in.
Cylinders 4ft. by 9in.
Height to top of chimney 7ft. 9in.
Length over buffers 17ft. 2in.
Weight 5 tons 6 cwt

The only concession to comfort was that the wheels were of the Mansell type with wooden centres to reduce noise. There is no complete record of GAZELLE's

travels in Mr Burkitt's ownership but it is known to have reached Chesterfield on one occasion. GAZELLE was advertised for sale by T.W.Ward Ltd in 1910 and was purchased by Holman Stephens in February 1911 for use as an inspection engine on the Shropshire & Montgomeryshire Railway, which he was reconstructing at the time. After a short period of inspection service GAZELLE was sent away to W.G.Bagnall Ltd at Stafford for conversion to an 0-4-2WT. GAZELLE returned to the S & M.R. in July 1911 and continued in use as an inspection engine.

Although the S & M.R. 'main line' had reopened from Shrewsbury to Llanymynech in April 1911 the branch line from Kinnerley to Criggion had remained closed while a new viaduct was built over the River Severn at Melverley. The branch line was reopened for goods traffic in February 1912 and for passengers in August 1912. Traffic on the branch was rarely substantial and Stephens felt that GAZELLE could provide an adequate service when loadings were particularly light. The vicar of Criggion, Reverend R Brock, thought otherwise as his letter of complaint of 23rd November 1912 to the Board of Trade shows:

'I booked today my fare by the 3.57 train from Abbey Gate station to Criggion on the Shropshire & Montgomeryshire Rly. I rode to Kinnerley Junction by a properly equipped train. Proceeding to the branch to Criggion, I was put with another man and two women into the back part of an engine with only a screen between us and the fire - no roof and the sparks and smuts falling over us - one spark nearly got into my eye - with danger of being blinded - my clothes too injured by the same. I wish to know whether passengers can thus be treated and deceived - for the last time I came about a fortnight ago I was conveyed in a carriage as I have hitherto been. I have had occasion to use the Rly for my wife and daughter and friends from London and of course I cannot subject them to such risk and barbarous treatment.

If they cannot or will not serve proper accommodations through the journey, they should not be allowed to advertise it - there were carriages at the station (Kinnerley) and as an engine ran - a carriage could and should have been on the back.'

Stephens replied to the Board of Trade explaining the situation: *'I reply to your communication of 30th November and find that it is usual, owing to the slight*

'Gazelle' as delivered to the S&MLR stands at Kinnerley in 1911. The single driving wheel may appear massive but was still smaller than a 'Terrier's' wheels. The passenger 'compartment' at the rear does not even have a screen yet.

'Gazelle' displays the coupled wheels, cab and passenger 'cell' fitted by Bagnall - certainly not beautiful but very practical.

Left : The proportions look better in three quarter view! The oval plate on the central splasher reads 'Shropshire & Montgomeryshire Railway Company'. Most of the Stephens' lines fitted such plates during the First World War.

Below : 'Gazelle' and tram trailer at Kinnerley in the 1920s. Someone has polished up the brass beading and nameplate on the splasher - one suspects the photographer and his jauntily clad accomplice.

5

Above : Undated view of 'Gazelle' and tram at Kinnerley though the disembodied Ilfracombe cab to the right may yield a clue. Note Spartan protection offered to passengers in the 'cell'. Faint lettering on tram reveals S&MR. Photograph LGRP.

Left : Ready for a trip on the branch? There was a bay platform at Kinnerley but it was often filled with carriages and departures from the 'main line' platform face were not unusual. Photo taken August 1926. Photograph H.C. Casserley.

traffic on the branch in question, to uti- lise the services of the inspection engine for the afternoon train as the occasion arises, wind screens are provided and in view of the smallness of the traffic it is considered that the action is justifi- able.' W.F.Marwood, writing on behalf of the Board of Trade, did not agree: 'I am to state for the information of your

directors that it is considered that a proper carriage for the conveyance of passengers should be run on the train in question'.

The Board of Trade's instructions can hardly be considered as ambiguous but Stephens was not easily put off. GA- ZELLE was sent back to W.G.Bagnall to have a cab and a passenger compart-

ment fitted. Neither fitting was exactly a thing of beauty. The cab was distinctly utilitarian with a shallow curved roof and bereft of all ornamentation apart from a pair of round spectacle glasses at the front and a spindly whistle pro- truding from the roof. The passenger cabin had all the welcome appearance of a portable prison cell. It was fitted with round spectacle glasses at the front

'Gazelle' at Kinnerley August 1939, with the hybrid trailer - part tram chassis and part Wolseley Siddeley body. Photograph R.G. Jarvis.

and two small square windows at the rear. The original half height rear door was retained but the rest of the doorway remained open to the elements. Baggage could be carried on the roof which was surrounded by an incongruously ornamental pair of luggage rails. None of this did anything for GAZELLE's appearance since the passenger cabin was a foot or more shorter than the driver's cab and its roof was curved at a much sharper radius.

It is not entirely clear how often GAZELLE served as a miniature railmotor in this form. There appear to have been no more letters of complaint from the Criggion vicarage and it may well be that GAZELLE was only pressed into passenger service when absolutely necessary. In 1915 or 1916 a more acceptable solution to the problem of lightly loaded passenger services on the Criggion Branch was found in the purchase and adaptation of a horse tram. This is reputed to have come from the L.C.C. and was originally a doubledeck vehicle. The top deck, stairs and end platforms were removed and the running gear made suitable for operation on railway track. In this form it made an ideal light trailer for GAZELLE which is unlikely to have been capable of hauling a conventional carriage. Although the tramcar was fitted with brakes these were operated by means of large handwheels protruding from either end of the carriage body and it is likely that these were only used to keep the vehicle from running away when parked on its own. Entrance was by means of end

doors and steps were provided between the buffers to assist access from the trackbed. A large lantern housing was retained at either end. The tramcar became No. 16 in the Shropshire & Montgomeryshire stocklist.

The idea of using a tramcar in this way was almost certainly borrowed from the narrow gauge Torrington & Marland Railway which had adapted two such cars, also reputedly from the L.C.C., in 1909. Stephens travelled on this line in August 1909 in connection with his application for the North Devon & Cornwall Junction Light Railway Order in November that year. The Torrington & Marland cars were slightly smaller than No. 16 and retained short end platforms so that they could be entered from the lineside.

GAZELLE and the tramcar continued to operate the Criggion Branch passenger service until the late 1920s. By October 1928 a service was only operating on Saturdays and by October 1932 this was only running as far as Melverley because of subsidence to the piers of Melverley viaduct. However, by this date GAZELLE had been taken out of service and the tramcar relegated to a siding at Kinnerley. There does not appear to be any record of when GAZELLE and the tramcar were taken out of service nor of the means by which the Criggion passenger service was provided in their absence, though it is possible that the S & M.R.'s Ford railmotor set was used between trips on the 'main line'. By May 1932 GAZELLE had been partially stripped down in Kinnerley

yard but it was unclear to visitors whether it was ever to be put together again. However, in 1936 W.H.Austen decided to reinstate it as an inspection engine. A complete overhaul then took place and in June 1937 it emerged from the Kinnerley repair shop in olive green paintwork complete with polished dome, safety valve and nameplates. To accompany it a railmotor body was united with the tramcar's running gear to form a new inspection saloon as described in a later chapter. GAZELLE thus survived to serve the armed forces during their occupation of the Shropshire & Montgomeryshire Railway and was particularly valuable for running early morning patrols along the line to detect acts of sabotage. The passenger cabin was removed during this period and GAZELLE would often run with the S & M.R. Royal Saloon if passengers needed to be carried, as the rebuilt inspection saloon had been taken out of service.

Although the Ministry of Defence continued to operate the Shropshire & Montgomeryshire until 1960 GAZELLE had left the line in 1950, to be preserved beside the parade ground at Longmoor Camp. When Longmoor was itself closed in 1970 GAZELLE moved on to the National Railway Museum at York and can now be seen at the Museum of Army Transport at Beverley. Its passenger cabin has not been reinstated and the uninitiated observer would have great difficulty in recognising it as a passenger carrying vehicle.

THE DREWRY CARS

Busy time at Clevedon - with only one platform the inter-connection of trains was a complicated matter. Ironically the waiting 'Terrier', No.2 'Portishead', was a later acquisition than the Drewry car or its trailer - a reminder that the railmotors were unsuitable for heavy traffic. Photo taken 1927. Photograph Rail Archive Stephenson.

Two petrol railmotors were acquired to operate on the Weston Clevedon & Portishead Railway and both were built by the Drewry Car Company Ltd. There were major differences between the two but as both were quite unlike any others on the Stephens railways we shall deal with them together.

The first Drewry, Works No.1252, was purchased in October 1921. It was four wheeled and could be driven from either end; powered by a Baguley four cylinder petrol engine its gearbox gave three speeds in either forward or reverse. Its main dimensions were:

Length over body 19ft. 0in.
Width 8ft. 0in.
Height above rail level 8ft. 3in.
Wheel diameter 2ft. 0in.
Weight in working order 6 tons
Seating 30 third class 12 standing

Radiators were fitted beneath the substantial buffer beams at each end, which were also fitted with side buffers at normal height and central three link couplings. Screw couplings later replaced these. A lamp bracket was fitted to the right of the coupling at one end and to the left at the other. On the other side of the coupling at each end a ladder was fitted to give access to the roof, which was fitted all round with a single luggage rail with ornamental curved ends at each corner.

The body was made of three-ply wooden panels covered with thin steel sheeting. There were three large windows on either side which could be dropped to their full depth for ample ventilation and three large windows in each end. Doors were fitted at both ends

of each side and steps were fitted beneath these for access from ground level, or from the low platforms used on this line - but hand rails to help the intending passenger were only provided above waist level. Six pairs of wooden slat seats with reversible tramcar-style backs were provided on either side of a central gangway together with two bench seats (for three persons) each fixed to the end bulkheads alongside the driver's position.

Most accounts of this railmotor describe it as being painted dark green with yellow lining but these colours are not usually associated with the Stephens regime of the early 1920s. It is possible that it was painted brown when delivered and that the green livery came at a later date. In its early days its ownership was shown by a circular garter device bearing the Railway's title on the centre of each side. In later years this was replaced by the initials W C & P R above the numeral 1 although it seems that the numeral was added later and that it ran for some time with only the initials.

A number of other alterations took place over the years. The original acetylene lighting was replaced by electric lighting and the opportunity was taken to fit an electric headlight above the centre of the waistline at each end. This must have improved safety when running after dark but an even greater safety improvement was achieved by removing the original internal petrol tank and replacing it with an external tank. The new tank was cylindrical and was fitted horizontally between the

buffer beam and waistline on the end of the vehicle. At the same time the exhaust pipe was carried up the other end of the vehicle above roof level and fitted with a hinged spring-loaded whistle. By pulling a control wire inside the vehicle the driver could position the whistle over the exhaust, where it would warble away to give warning of the railmotor's approach at the line's many level crossings.

The railmotor seems to have been a considerable success. The July 1922 timetable shows that it ran the 9.33 service from Clevedon to Weston Super Mare and the return service at 10.15, the 12.35 to Weston and the 1.15 back to Clevedon, the 3.15 from Clevedon to Portishead, the 3.52 from Portishead to Weston and a final 5.20 run from Weston to Clevedon. After 1927 railmotor mileage exceeded locomotive mileage on the W.C.& P.R.

The railmotor's capacity was often insufficient for the passenger traffic and a trailer carriage was therefore purchased from Drewry. This was their Works No.1323 and was delivered on 23rd March 1923. This seated 24 passengers and weighed 3 tons 5 cwts. It originally had open sides above the waistline with canvas curtains for protection against the elements. At an early date it was fitted with full height doors and the rest of the sides were panelled in with two large windows on either side. The upper halves of the windows in the doors were fixed panes but the lower halves could be lifted up for access to the external door handles. The side windows had inwardly hinged toplights.

The first Drewry car and its trailer, in the later style of livery. The motor has its petrol tank located above the buffer beam and the trailer has been glazed.

The ends of the trailer were fitted with two large windows from the start. There was no provision for operating the powered railmotor from the trailer so that the power car had to run round the trailer at each end of the line.

The trailer was fitted with substantial buffer beams and conventional buffers like the railmotor. It was equipped with screw couplings from the start but lamp brackets were not fitted until after delivery. No luggage rail or ladders were fitted and the steps beneath the doorways were of slightly lighter construction than those fitted to the railmotor. Outside axle boxes with conventional leaf springs were fitted, whereas the suspension of the railmotor remained a mystery, hidden away behind the wheels. It is believed that electric lighting was fitted to the trailer with power supplied by a jump cable from the railmotor. The trailer's livery seems to have gone through the same transformations as the railmotor except that no running number ever seems to have been applied.

A small wagon was supplied to run with the railmotor in 1925 but this will be dealt with in a later chapter. In 1934 an opportunity arose to purchase a second Drewry four wheeled railmotor, Works No.1650. This had been ordered by the Southern Railway in 1927 at a cost of £1,810 as an experiment to reduce the costs of branch line operations. This was delivered to the Southern in March 1928 and was a much more substantial vehicle than the W.C

& P.R. railmotor. Weighing in at 10 tons 17 cwts it was of normal height and had a wheelbase of 20 feet. A 50 h.p. petrol engine was fitted with its radiator mounted prominently on the end of the body. Three speed gears operated in both forward and reverse, as on the earlier railmotor.

The driver had his own cab at each end, that at the powered end having its own side doors. Behind this cab was a passenger compartment originally accommodating 26 passengers on moquette upholstered seats with reversible backs. Passengers entered by a doorway slightly over halfway along the body. Beyond this was a luggage compartment, equipped with double doors and accessible by a sliding door from the passenger compartment. Beyond

The first Drewry motor viewed from the Weston end. Note the whistle attached to the exhaust and the generous ventilation on a fine day.

this was the further driving cab which could only be entered from the luggage compartment. The doors to the passenger compartment were fitted with steps three treads deep whilst the driver's doors and luggage compartment doors only had double tread steps.

Views from this railmotor were not quite so panoramic as from its predecessor, for passengers had no forward or backward view, although the five side windows with inwardly hinged toplights provided quite a good outlook. Roof ventilators were also fitted and the windows in the passenger doors could be dropped to their full depth for additional fresh air on hot days. The driver's compartments were fitted with two forward windows separated by a large central panel and by side windows which could be dropped to full depth. The right hand window at each end was fitted with a windscreen wiper mounted at the base of the window.

Internal illumination was provided by electric lighting when delivered and the Southern subsequently fitted a single headlight, below the roofline at the centre of each end. Three lamp brackets were fitted along the top edge of the buffer beam. At the powered end only a coupling hook seems to have been provided but the other end was fitted with a three link coupling. Screw couplings do not ever seem to have been fitted to this railmotor.

The exterior of the bodywork was very plain but the Southern made up for this by lining it out to simulate panelling. Above the driver's side window at the unpowered end was painted the railmotor's running number, 5, and the words SOUTHERN and RAILWAY appeared at the same level on either side of the luggage doors. The Southern tried out the railmotor between Andover and Romsey in 1927, between Reading and Blackwater in 1928 and on the New Romney Branch in 1929. The following year it was taken into Ashford Works, a Parsons M4 64 h.p. engine fit-

The first Drewry waits at Weston in its original livery and loaded to capacity.

ted and seating reduced to 22, possibly by increasing the size of the luggage compartment. No.5's remaining service with the Southern seems to have been spent operating the New Romney Branch. In 1934 W.H.Austen purchased the railmotor from the Southern for £272 and it was delivered to Portishead in July. Little effort was made to alter the railmotor's appearance. It kept its coat of Southern green and its number 5. The words SOUTHERN and RAILWAY were painted over and RAILWAY's place was taken by W.C.& P.. With two railmotors in serv-

A clearer view of the early livery in 1927. Electric headlamps have been fitted since the previous photograph. Photograph Rail Archive Stephenson.

11

Between services at Clevedon in 1938. The luggage rails seem to have been taking some punishment. Despite the provision of sturdy ladders at each end nobody seems to have left their luggage on the roof. Photograph H.C. Casserley.

The second Drewry at Weston, showing its modified Southern livery. The oil lamp presumably acted as tail lamp when running after dark. Note the absence of exterior doors to the driver's cab at this end. The driving position is behind the window equipped with a wiper. Photograph Dr. Ian C. Allen.

The big Drewry stands at Clevedon on 13th July 1935. It must have been a hot day as every window that can be opened has been - including the unusual side-hung window in the front of the driver's cab. Photograph S.W. Baker.

The trailer made an odd sight attached to the big Drewry but seems to have been popular with the passengers. Note internal details of hinged toplights and the fixed upper panes in the doors. Weston, 7th April 1939. The railcar has been turned round at some time but exactly when and where is not clear.

The first Drewry in its final livery, complete with running number, at Clevedon on 25th June 1938. Photograph H.C. Casserley.

ice considerable savings were possible by reducing locomotive mileage, although a certain amount of steam mileage was still necessary for the Railway's mixed passenger and goods traffic. The larger railmotor's seating accommodation was less than that of the original railmotor and it was not uncommon to see the trailer car attached to No.5. The difference in roof levels presented quite a bizarre sight.

Unfortunately the fortunes of the Weston Clevedon & Portishead depended less on the seasonal passenger traffic than on the quarry traffic along the line. In 1939 this had dwindled to such an extent that closure seemed unavoidable. Traffic actually ceased on 18th May 1940 but in June 1940 the Great Western Railway purchased the rights of the Excess Insurance Company, the main creditor, in the line. The Great Western's motivation was not to operate the line but to use it for the storage of coal wagons rendered surplus by the cessation of exports to Europe. Nevertheless the Great Western's purchase included the Railway's rolling stock. The larger railmotor was marshalled in a train of W.C. & P.R. carriages and travelled to Swindon on its own wheels. The original railmotor and the trailer travelled to Swindon on well wagons. The body of the larger railmotor was purchased by a Swindon girls school for use as a pavilion but the other vehicles were broken up for scrap.

The big Drewry approaching Clevedon station with its number clearly inscribed in traditional locomotive style across the buffer beam. Photograph R.C. Riley Collection (on loan from Colonel Stephens Railway Museum).

Chapter Four
THE WOLSELEY-SIDDELEY AND THE FORD RAIL LORRY

The Wolseley Siddeley being delivered to Chichester. The motorcar bonnet is dwarfed by the bodywork. Note the absence of such sophistication as headlights, buffer beam or mudguards.

The period after the First World War was a difficult time for rural railways. Wages and the costs of materials had risen during the War and the sale of war surplus materials had unleashed at bargain prices large numbers of motor vehicles - which could carry local commercial traffic previously travelling by rail. The war years had also seen considerable improvements in the internal combustion engine which in turn enabled reliable local motor bus services to compete seriously with the railways for local passenger traffic. Faced with increased costs and declining traffic the railways had to find some way of retrieving the situation.

Popular solutions were : to reduce services or to operate motor bus services of their own. The North Eastern Railway, however, decided to convert a Leyland motor bus to operate on rails. This was not an entirely new idea. The Caledonian Railway had previously converted a motor charabanc to operate its Connel Ferry service in 1911. The North Eastern's experiment was different in that their Leyland bus was adapted to operate in either direction, thus avoiding any need to install turntables or turning triangles at the ends of the lines

over which it was used. The experiment was reported briefly in RAILWAY GAZETTE in 1921. The bus, N.E.R. No.110, was described as a Leyland 35 h.p. model seating 26 and it was operating in the York - Copmanthorpe - Strensall - Earswick area. In 1923 it was transferred to Selby, where it continued to operate until destroyed by fire in 1926.

We have no evidence to confirm that Holman Stephens was directly influenced by the North Eastern Railway experiment but it seems more than a coincidence that it was about this time that he built a very similar vehicle. The first evidence for the construction of this railmotor is a photograph found on the premises of Drake & Fletcher, motor engineers of Maidstone. The photograph is unfortunately not dated and Drake & Fletcher had no other record or recollection of the vehicle. The photograph shows a Wolseley-Siddeley motor car chassis fitted with rail wheels and carrying what appears to be the body of a platelayer's trolley, lettered K & E S R. The chassis seems to have been lengthened and a second radiator has been fitted at the back, presumably for cooling when running in reverse.

The chassis has a chain drive. Wolseley and Siddeley worked together building motorcars from 1904 to 1910 but abandoned chain drives in 1909. The chassis is therefore from an old motorcar rather than from a current model. Since the photograph was found at a motor engineer's premises it seems probable that the basic conversion work was carried out by them, although the flanged disc wheels may have been fitted by the Kent & East Sussex. Unfortunately the Kent & East Sussex records are as silent on the subject as Drake & Fletcher's.

The chassis was then fitted with a passenger body at Rolvenden. There is a tantalising glimpse of what appears to be the body under construction, in the background of an undated photograph of 0-8-0T HECATE, but reliable reports testify to its construction 'in a cow shed in Vale Road, Tonbridge' and the scene at Rolvenden was presumably its attachment to the prepared chassis. Official photographs of the completed vehicle were then taken at Rolvenden and it must be presumed that the railmotor at least ran trials on the Kent & East Sussex. The next known photograph of the Wolseley-

15

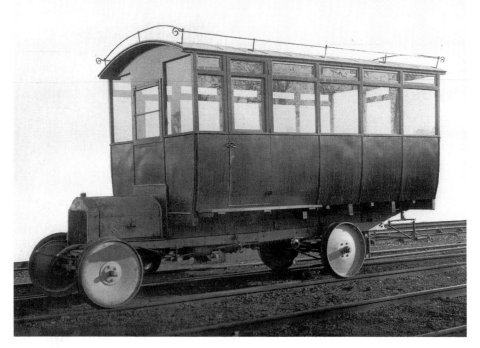

Left : Official photograph of the Wolseley Siddeley showing the chain drive to the rear axle. Note the short footboard and the general absence of decorative features, apart from the elegant luggage rail fittings. Photograph Colonel Stephens Railway Museum.

Right : Wolseley Siddeley, as delivered to the S&MR, stands at Kinnerley with the tram trailer it is destined to replace. Photograph Lens of Sutton.

Left : The Wolseley Siddeley body in departmental use at Chapel Lane, Kinnerley on 21st September 1958. It remained here, outlasting the railway, until removed for preservation.

16

Siddeley, again undated, shows it being unloaded from a well wagon on to the Selsey Tramway at Chichester and it seems to have spent some time on this line. There is only one other photograph that we know of showing it on the Selsey Tramway, dated July 1927, but the railmotor was clearly remembered by Herbert Warwick, who drove on the Tramway from 1923 to 1926. He recollected that it was extremely difficult to start and that the rear radiator was smashed when the railmotor was being turned on the Southern turntable at Chichester. Although the railmotor appears to have been capable of running in either direction it is not clear whether there were actually any controls at the rear. The thought of passengers rattling backwards along the makeshift track of the Selsey Tramway with the driver keeping a lookout over his shoulder is not for the faint of heart!

At an unknown date, hopefully fairly soon after the arrival of the Wolseley-Siddeley, Stephens acquired a Ford motor lorry, fitted it with flanged wheels and coupled it back to back with the railmotor. The rail lorry could then pull the Wolseley-Siddeley in one direction and the Wolseley-Siddeley could pull the rail lorry in the other direction... Above all the driver could always be at the front of whichever vehicle was leading.

Even less is known about the Ford rail lorry than about the Wolseley-Siddeley. It has usually been described as a Model T but this seems to be due more to the association of that description with any antiquated Ford vehicle than to any serious knowledge of its actual type. At an unrecorded date, probably 1928,* the Wolseley-Siddeley and the Ford rail lorry left the Selsey Tramway for the Shropshire & Montgomeryshire Railway. The S & M.R. do not seem to have had any immediate use for the Wolseley-Siddeley, which appears to have been relegated to the dump siding at Kinnerley, in the hope that it might come in useful some day. The Ford rail lorry was occasionally put to use with one or other of the Ford railmotors but was also consigned to the dump siding in the early 1930s, subsequently disappearing without trace. Neither vehicle ever appeared in the S & M.R.'s official returns but the Railway Year Book did include an entry for '1 goods truck' from 1934 to 1937 which may have been a belated reference to the rail lorry, as freight vehicles were reported separately.

In 1934 R.W. Kidner found the Wolseley-Siddeley at Kinnerley 'in a poor state' and contemporary photographs suggest that this was something of an understatement. However, Austen's decision to reinstate GAZELLE as an inspection engine in 1937 led to the body being removed from the Wolseley-Siddeley and fitted to the underframe of tramcar 16, to provide a light inspection saloon that would not unduly tax GAZELLE's hauling powers. GAZELLE and its trailer were also available for private hire and received considerable publicity amongst railway enthusiasts when hired by the Birmingham Locomotive Club for a trip over the line in April 1939.

During the Second World War the trailer's chassis is reported to have 'broken its back'. Once again the body was removed and put into use as a platelayer's hut alongside the Criggion Branch at Kinnerley and here it survived the closure of the Railway. In 1975 it was measured up and found to be approximately 14ft. long by 7ft. wide and 7ft. high. The wooden body frame was clad in steel below the waist but no trace remained of any internal fittings or original paintwork. It was felt at the time that what remained of the body was beyond repair and would soon disintegrate but a visit in 1987 found the remains sufficiently intact to justify an attempt at preservation. The body has since been removed to Bicton Heath and may yet resume something of its earlier appearance. Now if someone knows the whereabouts of a suitable Wolseley-Siddeley chassis...

*The choice of 1928 is based on the Selsey Tramway's entries in the Railway Year Book. These show '4 Rail Motors' for each year from 1925 to 1932. As a pair of Shefflex railmotors were acquired in 1928 it is possible that these displaced the Wolseley-Siddeley/Ford rail lorry combination. It must be emphasised that Railway Year Book entries, although more accurate than those in the Universal Directory of Railway Officials, cannot be taken as gospel. We have not found any official returns for the Tramway before 1929.

The Ford rail lorry back-to-back with the Wolseley Siddeley in Selsey shed. This rare image was discovered as a magic lantern slide in Cornwall! Photograph Colonel Stephens Railway Museum.

THE FORD RAILMOTORS

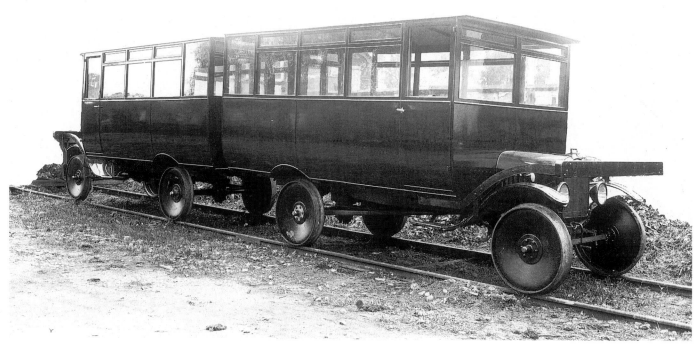

Official photograph of the first KESR Ford set. Footboards were yet to be fitted and the headlamps and mud guard-mounted sidelights were not destined to become permanent features. Photograph Colonel Stephens Railway Museum.

American railways appreciated the advantages of internal combustion at an earlier date than their British counterparts. In recognition of this the Ford Motor Company marketed their 'Supaphord' gear box as particularly suitable in constructing light petrol rail units from commercial road motor components. It was therefore possible for railways or railway engineering businesses to buy kits of parts to make up railmotor units to their own specifications. Although these railmotors would contain large numbers of components that would also be found in contemporary road vehicles, it is important to note that they were not converted road vehicles, as has often been assumed.

Stephens was quick to appreciate the advantages offered by this form of railmotor; it was comparatively cheap to purchase and many of the spare parts could be obtained from a local garage. Stephens purchased four pairs of these railmotors and attempted to buy a fifth pair, the only other examples of this type of railmotor known to

have been used in Britain. In America, where turntables and turning triangles were more common as a result of the

widespread operation of tender locomotives on branch lines, it was common practice for this type of railmotor to run

Later view of first KESR set at Biddenden. Footboards now fitted and a safer place has been found for the headlight. Photograph Kent Messenger.

The first KESR Ford unit approaches Rolvenden - date unknown but probably late 1920s. Photograph Stephen Garrett Collection.

as a single unit. For Stephens' purposes it made more sense to buy pairs of railmotors, couple them back to back and let the leading car haul the other as a trailer with its gears in neutral. Fortunately somebody had the foresight to include a locking mechanism to prevent youthful passengers from engaging the gears when travelling unsupervised in the trailing car.

KENT & EAST SUSSEX FORD No.1

Stephens' first pair of Ford railmotors appears to have been delivered to the Kent & East Sussex in 1923 from Edmonds of Thetford, though the bodywork had been sub-contracted to Eton Coachworks of Cringleford. Later documents refer to these railmotors as having been built and purchased in 1922 but the first clearly dated reference to them is a manuscript note recording eight failures in service between February and May 1923 and a short article in *Locomotive Magazine* on 14th April 1923 suggests that they had been delivered in that year.

This pair of railmotors differed slightly in bodywork from the later models although the seating capacity of 20 in each car was the same. The basic structure consisted of a typical Ford bonnet and mudguards protruding from a box-shaped body, sides curving in neatly below the waist and a shallow curved roof. The roof curved down to end flush with the body at the front and back and was not fitted with luggage rails. A running board extended the full length of each side of the body but the wheel arch for the rear wheels curved up above the

Early view of KESR first Ford set at Tenterden Town with later buffing bar but original lighting.

running board. The front of the body above the waistline was divided into two windows, with toplights which seem to have been able to hinge inwards for ventilation. Doors were positioned at the leading edge of the body side and had drop windows. Three windows with hinged toplights and one window without a toplight extended from the door to the back of the body. At least one of the non-toplight windows was subsequently replaced by a window with toplight but it is not clear if this was fixed or opening. The set seems to have been painted dark brown when delivered but this faded over the years to a rather anaemic buff colour.

The pair was delivered with headlights attached to either side of the bonnet. Subsequently one of these headlights was taken away and later still the remaining headlight was moved to the centre of the roofline. Another alteration made was to the buffer bar. Originally there was a sort of perambulator handle arrangement, with two fairly sturdy curved side pieces ending in small square buffing blocks which were connected across the front of the bonnet by a rather ineffectual rod. The buffing blocks and rod were subsequently replaced by a solid bar.

No photographs have come to light showing the back of these railmotors, or the arrangements for coupling them together, but it seems likely that there were sliding doors, allowing passage between the two cars and the same sort of slotted block coupling used on the other Fords. No couplings were ever fit-ted to the outer ends of this railmotor set. Plain disc wheels were fitted and seem to have been retained throughout its service on the line.

On 14th April 1923 *Locomotive Magazine* published the following short article which did much to create the misunderstanding that the Ford railmotors were converted road vehicles:

PETROL RAIL MOTORS
KENT AND EAST SUSSEX RAILWAY

Between Robertsbridge and Headcorn the Kent & East Sussex Ry. now convey passengers by two Ford cars placed back to back and coupled together. The original road wheels have been replaced by flanged wheels.

Colonel H.F.Stephens, the managing director of the Kent & East Sussex line, informs us that the petrol consumption for the 24 miles run, with gradients of 1 in 50, is only 1 3/4 gallons with a full load.'

There are few records of the actual operation of this set, used on both the Headcorn and Robertsbridge sections of the line. Local memory has it that when it arrived at Rolvenden on its inaugural run there was some consternation when it was found that the doors fouled the platform edge and would not open. Since there are no signs of subsequent alteration to either the railmotors or the platform it must be presumed that the set had pulled up alongside the raised section for loading milk churns, and that the problem was resolved by running forward to the lower portion beyond. In its first year of operation this railmotor set ran 20,540 miles.

Subsequent Kent & East Sussex records do not make any distinction between this set and a second which was obtained the following year. Both seem to have enjoyed the same strengths and weaknesses as their fellow Fords. On the credit side they were cheap to operate and did not spend time shunting goods wagons at intermediate stations as the locomotive-hauled mixed trains did. Their disadvantages were noise, vibration and mechanical breakdown. These disadvantages seem to have become more apparent in the railmotors' later years, heightened by the obvious disapproval of railway enthusiasts who had visited the line in search of vintage steam. The railmotors certainly had one admirer in the novelist Sheila Kaye-Smith, who included the following passage in *Ember Lane* published in 1940:

'The passengers travelled democratically in a classless vehicle made of two motor-omnibuses set end to end on a railway chassis, and driven by a sort of chauffeur/engine driver seated under the floor, his head on a level with the traveller's knees.'

Whilst the driver's position was certainly set at a lower level than that of the passengers, this description is somewhat exaggerated. There is no complaint made against the comfort of the ride though it is described as a 'merry bounce' - which may not have been to every passenger's liking.

First Ford set running through the hop fields near Rolvenden in September 1923 with original buffing bar. The bonnet seems to have been loosened to provide extra cooling. LCGB, Ken Nunn collection.

Official view of the Shropshire & Montgomeryshire 3 car set. The fate of the centre car is something of a mystery as it only appears in very early photographs of the set. Photograph Colonel Stephens Railway Museum.

In July 1932 W.H.Austen sought permission from the Chancery Division to dispose of this railmotor set:

'The Number 1 set petrol rail cars... are in a very bad condition and beyond repair but some parts thereof could be used as spare parts for the Number 2 petrol rail car set of the Respondent Company which is still in use.'

Obviously permission was granted as a subsequent note records that one body of 'No.1 Set Rail Cars' was sold on 30th July 1932 for £1.10.0. The other car lingered on for some time until a further note recorded: 'One Body No.1 sold to Hills for 10/-. Paid in 26/1/35.'

SHROPSHIRE & MONGOMERYSHIRE FORD SET

The S & M.R. acquired a Ford set in 1923 from Edmonds of Thetford. This differed from the other Edmonds sets in that it was a three car unit with a central unpowered trailer. The body style of the powered units set the pattern for the other units supplied by Edmonds. The standard Ford bonnet and mudguards were retained on the front of a box body with the sides curving in beneath the waistline. Running boards ran the full length of the body without any visible wheel arch for the rear wheels. The body front had three equal sized windows, with hinged toplights above. Along the body side came a very narrow window, six inches wide at most, with fixed toplight, outward opening door with fixed toplight and drop window, and four equal sized windows with inwardly hinged toplights. At the back was a central sliding door with fixed toplight and vertical handrails below the waistline on either side of the doorway, which was also flanked by windows with toplights.

The roof maintained a shallow curve throughout its length and slightly overhung the front of the car. Slats were fixed longitudinally along the roof and a single luggage rail with ornamental corners ran round the whole of the roof.

A straight buffer bar was supported in front of the radiator by two steel rods on either side, one fixed at an angle to the lower corner of the body and the other at an angle to the engine mounting. Two headlights were fitted, one on either side of the radiator. There were no couplings at the outer ends. Plain disc wheels were fitted.

The body style of the trailer was virtually identical to that of the power cars, except for the absence of the narrow leading side window and the fitting of a central door. The capacity of the trailer was 20, the same as the powered cars. Seating in all three cars appears to have been on wooden slatted seats with reversible backs.

Alterations were made to the cars over the years. Klaxon horns were fitted which protruded from the front of the powered cars. Large tool boxes were fitted above the running board behind the right hand doors of the powered cars. Presumably more tools were needed as the unit aged, because a second tool box was fitted beneath the running board on the left hand side of the power cars, and for a time a rack for petrol cans was fitted beneath the running board on the right hand side of the powered car, at the Shrewsbury end of the unit.

The rod supports for the buffer bar seem to have been inadequate and were replaced by curved 'pram handle' bars parallel to the bonnet sides. For a while at least one of the powered cars ran without a buffer bar. The buffer bars themselves had small oblong buffing blocks added to their outer ends though it is questionable whether these added any real degree of safety. In their final years a lamp bracket was fixed to the centre of the buffer bars. This followed the removal of one headlight at a fairly early date and the later disconnection or extinction of the other. The original plain disc wheels seem to have alternated with three hole disc wheels - the

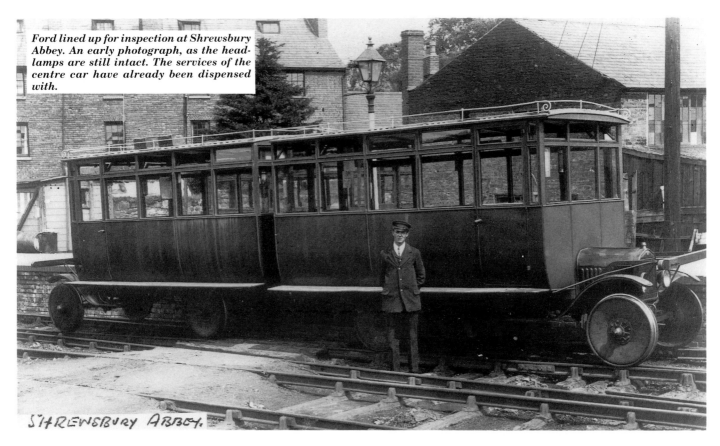

SHREWSBURY ABBEY.

number of different combinations of wheels seen in photographs attests to a high frequency of wheel changes.

The *Locomotive Magazine* reported the introduction of this railmotor set in its issue of 15th September 1923:

'RAIL MOTORS SHROPSHIRE AND MONTGOMERYSHIRE RY.

'For passenger service a three car motor train ... has been put into traffic by Col.H.F.Stephens, on the Shropshire & Montgomeryshire Railway (Shrewsbury to Llanymynech). These interesting adaptations of road motors for rail service are arranged back to back, with an intermediate dummy car in the centre, giving accommodation in all for sixty passengers. Light passenger bodies have been fitted on the motor car frames, the usual steering gear dismantled, and flanged wheels fitted to solid axles. A sliding door at the rear of each body provides access to the centre car. Centre drawpin connections are used for coupling the cars.

'The train maintains a good average speed, the economical rate being about 25 miles per hour, but it will run faster. It will climb gradients of 1 in 50 with 9 chains curves quite easily, and manage long stretches of 1 in 130 and 1 in 150 without overheating. It is early to give figures at present, but on trial the train ran 50 miles on 7 gallons of petrol with three cars, or working as a two-car unit just over 1 1/2 gallons of petrol for 18 miles, the load being made up with bags of

coal, etc., to the full complement of passengers. When running the gear of the rear car is placed in neutral.'

Little more was recorded of the service of the railmotor unit in its early years. There are very few photographs showing the set running with the trailer; this has led to suggestions that the set had insufficient power to run with all three vehicles fully loaded but there is no official record to support this. After the arrival of the Ford rail lorry from the Selsey Tramway some services were operated by one of the Edmonds powered cars, coupled to the rail lorry. This would have enabled services to be maintained when one of the powered cars needed overhaul.

An entry in the Directors' Minute Book for 23rd September 1930 recorded that the railcars had been de-

S&MR set at Llanymynech. This view is sometimes described as showing all three cars but the 'third car' is actually the open door from which the young lady has emerged. Both headlamps still in place but only one seems to be in operating condition. Photograph LGRP.

S&MR set in its usual 2 car formation. Alterations since delivery include the fitting of boxes and racks to the footboard, addition of klaxon and loss of one headlight. Photographed at Kinnerley in 1931.

railed and badly damaged, and that the line was being entirely worked by steam . A further entry on 26th November recorded that the railcar driver had been dismissed and that the Railway might dispense with railcars altogether. It is significant that the intermediate trailer was withdrawn in 1930, though whether this was to provide parts for the repair of the powered cars or because it had suffered irreparable damage is not clear. It may simply have been surplus to the line's requirements by this date.

The Directors decided not to dispense with the railmotors and they had returned to service by March 1931 when it was reported that they were using more petrol even though they were running fewer services. This led to further consideration of their future and it was decided on 29th April 1932 to discontinue their use and to dismiss the railcar driver, Mr S Nevett. Mixed trains would operate all services from 30th April. However, a falling off in the Criggion stone traffic and a shortage of serviceable locomotives led the Directors to relent at their meeting on 28th November 1932 when they agreed to allow the railcars to run 'if necessary'.

Regular passenger services ended on the S & M.R. in November 1933 but the railmotors remained available for occasional excursions and the

limited services that ran on bank holidays. When even the holiday services were withdrawn in 1937 the railmotors were set aside for the last time. They appear to have been broken up early in the Second World War.

KENT & EAST SUSSEX
FORD SET No 2

The Kent & East Sussex must have been satisfied with their first pair of railmotors because they purchased a

second set in 1924. Although the Railway's records clearly refer to this railmotor set as No 2 there is no record of either of the Ford sets ever being lettered with their running numbers. The new set's bodywork was identical to that of the S & M.R. powered cars although the K & E.S.R. appear to have been somewhat confused as to the seating capacity of their new set. The first set had been credited with 40 seats but the arrival of the new set only increased the

The Ford set lingered for many years in the Kinnerley yard after the closure of passenger services.

The second KESR set in brand new condition at Tenterden Town. The sidelights on the mudguards were soon to disappear. The driver's position seems to offer minimum visibility. Photograph R.M. Jones Collection.

Railway's railmotor seating total to 70.

Some of the subsequent alterations to this set were also the same as those practised on the S & M.R.. The original plain disc wheels gave way to the three hole pattern and the pair of bonnet-mounted headlights were eventually replaced by one headlight mounted on the roof. However, the K & E.S.R. No 2 set distinguished itself from all the other Fords by having its buffer bars replaced by a sturdy buffer arrangement at axle level. This had a central drop pin coupling fitted for attaching a light baggage trailer, apparently supplied with a later Shefflex railmotor set. On either side of the coupling were two small hooks, presumably for additional coupling chains,

'Everybody change places!'. The ways of photographers can be strange but nobody seems to be complaining in this informative view. The sliding doors put paid to the Kent & East Sussex tradition of ticket collectors moving from carriage to carriage on the outside of the train. Photograph Colonel Stephens Railway Museum.

Another early view of the second set, with the original headlamps intact. Note the rare instance of luggage on the roof, though the 'luggage' in this case is spare petrol cans. Photograph R.W. Kidner.

and at the outer ends of the buffer bars were two attachments which appear to have been intended to carry screw jacks.

The arrival of the second rail motor set during 1924 was particularly fortunate as the line was flooded on 2nd January 1925 and remained closed to normal traffic until the 6th January but the railmotors were able to resume services on 3rd January. One would not normally believe a low slung petrol railmotor to be more aquatic than a steam locomotive but the K & E.S.R. had had experience of 0-6-0ST No 8 HESPERUS losing its footing in flood-water and turning on its side. Presumably the light railmotor sets were less likely to displace the submerged track. The railmotor mileages from 1923 to 1937 were recorded separately from steam train mileages and although the following figures do not distinguish between the mileages of the two Ford sets

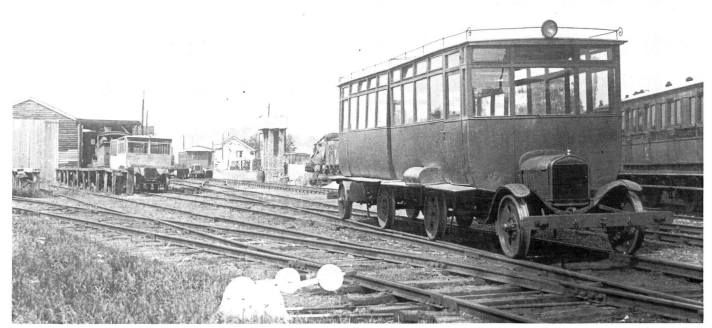

A rare view of all three KESR railmotor sets. Second Ford in right foreground, first Ford to the left and Shefflex at the platform. Photograph Colonel Stephens Railway Museum.

The diminutive size of the railmotors is brought out in this view of the second Ford set at Tenterden Town on 15th August 1931. The milk churns and luggage will have to wait for the next steam-hauled 'mixed'. Photograph LGRP.

and the Shefflex they give a clear picture of the important part played by railmotors in the operation of the Kent & East Sussex .

YEAR	STEAM MILEAGE	PETROL MILEAGE
1923	76,826	20,540
1924	71,946	28,413
1925	58,426	26,146
1926	39,420	43,308
1927	58,004	28,439
1928	51,460	29,382
1929	55,502	37,195
1930	47,380	33,810
1931	34,660	32,064
1932	32,062	12,418
1933	30,282	10,488
1934	30,756	14,604
1935	33,117	15,036
1936	35,074	14,317
1937	41,818	6,262

The figures for 1926 are particularly significant as it was the year of the Coal Strike and the availability of petrol vehicles obviously enabled services to be run for which fuel might otherwise not have been available.

The No.2 set last ran on 17th August 1937 but was not broken up for some time. One body was sold to a Mr Wiffen on the 1st August 1939 for 15/- and the other body seems to have been sold together with the Shefflex

bodies to a Mr Smith on the 8th August 1939. The Shefflex set was actually broken up before the No.2 set but this may simply have reflected the fact that the Shefflex was parked in front of the Ford. There is no record of the disposal of the running gear of any of the

railmotor sets but these were probably included in a number of sales of anonymous scrap metal at this time.

THE SELSEY TRAMWAY FORD SET
There is some mystery as to the date on which the Selsey Tramway acquired

Second Ford at Rolvenden. Note the drawbar, roof-mounted headlamp, toolbox and later pattern wheels.

Second Ford set at Rolvenden, flanked by the Hawthorn Leslie twins in 1932. Note the mystery implements attached to the fittings on each side of the drawbar. Photograph Dr. Ian C. Allen.

The Selsey Ford set caught in the loop platform at Tenterden Town, before delivery to Sussex. Note the beading round the waist panel, unique to this unit, and the curved spoke wheels. Photograph Colonel Stephens Railway Museum.

its pair of Ford railmotors. The date has often been given as 1923 but the first mention of railmotors in the Tramway's entry in the RAILWAY YEAR BOOK does not occur until 1925. The first photograph of the Selsey Ford set to which a date can confidently be ascribed is October 1925 and the Tramway's Capital Account for 1925 shows an increased expenditure on rolling stock of £2,148-7s-5d. Part of this sum would have been accounted for by payments for the 0-6-

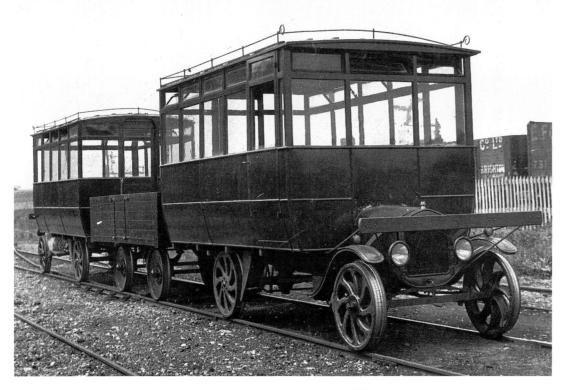

The unit has now reached Chichester and taken up company with its trailer. Note that the trailer is five planks high and the Ford cars, lacking drawgear at the outer ends, must travel between the two. Photograph Colonel Stephens Railway Museum.

Milk traffic at Chalder. The Selsey Tramway made much more use of their railmotors for light goods traffic than the other Stephens' lines. Photograph Collection S.R. Garrett.

Not the clearest of views but clear enough to show a Selsey phenomenon - the hybrid set; the leading railmotor is a Shefflex but the trailing unit is a Ford. Photograph John Scott Morgan Collection.

proving trials cannot now be said. The Selsey Ford set was almost identical in appearance to the Shropshire & Mongomeryshire powered cars as delivered. The only significant differences in appearance were that a line of beading was applied midway all round the lower bodywork except for the front panel over the bonnet, spoked wheels with eight curving spokes were used instead of disc wheels, and the roofs were covered with both lateral and longitudinal laths instead of just longitudinal laths. One new feature was the fitting of small sidelights on the mudguards in addition to the headlights fitted on either side of the bonnet.

Relatively few changes were made to the Selsey Fords. The buffer bar supports which were originally the same as those on the Shropshire Fords retained the outer steel rod angled from the bottom body corner but supplemented this with the curved 'pram handle' bars parallel to the bonnet with which the Shropshire cars were later fitted. The cars retained their two headlights until withdrawal though these do not appear to have functioned for some time. The side doors appear to have required attention at some point as they have lost their line of beading in later photographs. At some stage the spoked wheels at the powered ends of the cars were replaced by plain disc wheels.

It is possible that the Ford cars may have operated with the Ford rail lorry or Wolseley-Siddeley car from time to time. Whilst there is no evidence for this there is a good photograph of a Ford car running coupled to one of the later Shefflex cars at Selsey Bridge.

The Selsey Tramway went into receivership in 1931. In 1934 there was some hope that the Southern Railway would take over the line but the dubious legal position of the Tramway and its extremely run down condition persuaded

OST MOROUS from the Shropshire & Montgomeryshire Railway but since the S & M.R. were still seeking payment for this locomotive in 1931 and only considered as being 'on loan' to the Selsey line it is unlikely to have accounted for much of the expenditure. It is conceivable that the railmotors arrived earlier, having been paid for privately by Stephens, and that the Tramway did not take them into stock or pay for them until 1925. In the absence of reliable contemporary information this question must remain open. One final note of mystery concerning the delivery of this set is the existence of a photograph in the Kent & East Sussex Archives showing this set standing alongside the 'island' platform at Tenterden Town. Whether the set was diverted en route to the Selsey to stand in for one of the Kent & East Sussex sets or whether it went first to the Kent & East Sussex for

Some railways go out fighting, others fade away. In 1934 the Selsey Ford set was fading too.

29

Radiator topping up in progress at Chichester. No sign of passengers but the baggage trailer seems well loaded. Photograph Lens of Sutton.

The Ford unit in its final days at Selsey. Note the replacement wheels, doors without beading and the loss of the corner post on the rear car. Photograph Collection S.R. Garrett.

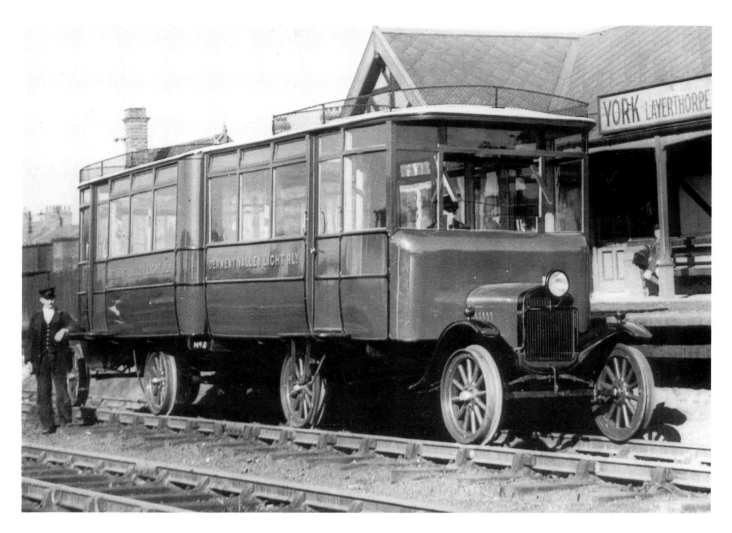

the Southern that the line was not a viable investment. The following comment was made in the Southern's report : 'The average speed of the rail motor service is 14.7 miles per hour, whilst the mixed train travels at an average speed of 10 miles per hour. Despite these low average speeds the trains are not infrequently late.' Services ceased on 19th January 1935 and the Ford railmotors were sold with the rest of the Tramway's stock to Mr F Watkins of Sling, Gloucestershire on 3rd March 1936. Mr Watkins subsequently auctioned much of the railway plant on 30th June 1936. There is no apparent record of the fate of the Ford cars but it is known that their bodies were removed from their chassis and it is possible that they saw further use as garden sheds.

THE DERWENT VALLEY FORD RAILMOTOR SET

This appears to have been the only other Ford railmotor set to have operated in England and was the subject of a lengthy article in RAILWAY GAZETTE on 21st November 1924. The Derwent Valley Railway had previously relied on conventional carriages hauled by locomotives hired from the North Eastern Railway. The absorption of the N.E.R.

into the London & North Eastern Railway had resulted in a steep rise in locomotive hire charges and the Derwent Valley had sought to cut their costs by investing £1,070 in a Ford railmotor set.

This Ford set was somewhat more elegant than those supplied by Edmonds and had bodywork supplied by Charles Roe (1923) Ltd of Leeds complete with the luxury of sprung upholstery. Each car seated 18 passengers and was based on a standard Ford 1 ton truck chassis. Two cars running together obtained 14.33 m.p.g. and a car running on its own obtained 17.55 mpg.

Unfortunately road motorbus competition made the railmotor service unprofitable and the Derwent Valley Railway suspended its passenger services in 1926. The railmotor set was put up for sale and attracted the attention of Holman Stephens who apparently intended to purchase it for the East Kent Railway. Unfortunately he was pipped at the post by George Glover of the County Donegal Railways Joint Committee which had already experimented with a very small petrol railmotor built by Allday & Onions but subsequently fitted with a Ford engine. Glover purchased the Derwent Valley set for £480 and converted it to 3ft. gauge for use as two single railmotors. They were not

Above : Every inch the de-luxe version when compared with the Stephens' Fords, the Derwent Valley set stands at York Layerthorpe. Photograph Rail Archive Stephenson.

particularly successful on the County Donegal and were both withdrawn in 1934. They had, however, convinced the County Donegal of the practicality of internal combustion railmotors and were succeeded by an increasingly sophisticated series of petrol and diesel units.

FORD RAILMOTORS IN NORTH WALES

There is considerable evidence that Stephens contemplated the use of Ford railmotors on the Festiniog and Welsh Highland Railways. There are references in the Festiniog Archives to a number of proposals made in 1923 to equip these lines with railmotors and rail lorries. The Archives also contain some Ford plans which were presumably obtained to assess the feasibility of such a scheme. Whether the scheme was dropped because of the relatively poor performance of the various petrol shunters tried out on the Festiniog and the Welsh Highland or for some other reason has gone unrecorded.

Chapter Six

THE SHEFFLEX CARS

The Selsey Shefflex set runs into Selsey Bridge Halt. The electric gong fitted after an accident in 1932 is apparent. Photograph Dr. Ian C. Allen.

The Festiniog Railway Archives contain the following advertisement placed in *Motor Transport* on 3rd January 1927: *'REQUIRED 2 good second-hand motor omnibuses, not less than 14 seaters, 4ft. 6in. - 5f.t wheel track. Write Col H.F. Stephens, Tonbridge.'*

Whilst it is unclear whether this advertisement indicates a renewal of interest in narrow gauge railmotor operation it is at least evidence that Stephens was contemplating the acquisition of further railmotors. The fact that he did obtain a railmotor set from a relatively unknown manufacturer later in 1927 suggests that he received at least one reply to his advertisement.

Stephens' new supplier was Shefflex Motors Limited of Sheffield whose main line of business was the construction of 30 cwt and 40 cwt lorries to a design which had first been manufactured under contract for Commer during the First World War. Not only were the prices charged by Sheffex considerably cheaper than those of other manufacturers but they

had also supplied some of their vehicles as motor buses. Their vehicles were not particularly sophisticated but they were solidly built and economical to run. With such a specification it is not surprising that Stephens found them a suitable proposition for a new generation of railmotors.

THE SELSEY SHEFFLEX SET

The Shefflex Motors order book allots chassis numbers 2058 and 2059 to the 'Shrops & Montgomeryshire Railway' on 14th December 1927. It is not clear whether this was a delivery date or an order date. It is even less clear how these vehicles came to be supplied to the Selsey Tramway instead of to the S & M.R. but this may explain the transfer of the Wolseley-Siddeley and Ford rail lorry from the Selsey to the S & M.R. by way of compensation. Although delivered to the Selsey Tramway and included in that Company's returns it must be noted that this railmotor set remained the personal property of Holman Stephens and was never pur-

chased by the Tramway. By this date the Tramway was usually known as the West Sussex Railway.

A long article describing this set was published in *Locomotive Magazine* on 15th February 1928 from which we have taken the following extracts :
'SHEFFLEX RAIL CAR, WEST SUSSEX RAILWAY
Satisfactory results have attended the trials of a new rail car which Lieut-Col H F Stephens has introduced on the passenger service of the West Sussex Railway (Chichester to Selsey), formerly the Hundred of Manhood and Selsey Tramway, but brought under the Railways Act by the Railways Construction and Facilities Act 1864, a very unusual proceeding. These cars have been built by the Shefflex Motor Co., of Tinsley, Sheffield.

As will be seen from the accompanying illustration, there are two cars, each seating 23 passengers, which usually run coupled together. The wheelbase is 11 ft. and the overall length of the frame 16 ft 8 in., plus front and rear

Shefflex set in brand new condition at Selsey Town showing the intricate lining out. Photo dated September 1928. Photograph Colonel Stephens Railway Museum.

The Shefflex runs into Selsey Town with faint vestiges of its original lining still visible. Note that the rear light is fitted to the left footboard at this end. Photograph Lens of Sutton.

buffers. Ball and roller bearings are used practically in every part of the chassis, while, in keeping with its place of origin, special steels are used where ordinarily mild steel would be employed.

Running empty, a steady speed of about 30 miles per hour can be maintained, and the ability to pick up from very low speeds on top gear is excellent..... A particularly noticeable feature of the engine is its quietness when idling .... The lighting system is C.A.V. with head and rear light, and also interior lights.

The bodies are built by Messrs. W.J.Flear Ltd., of Burton Road, Sheffield, with luggage rails fitted on the tops. Large plate-glass windows are provided above elbow level, ventilators being fitted above to admit air without draught. Throw-over, spring seats are arranged across the car, with a gangway down the centre. The carriages are warmed by hot-air pipes heated by the exhaust gases,

The Shefflex between services at Selsey Town. Note how the wheel tread overlaps the light section rails.

which are easily disconnected in warm weather. Exhaust whistles are fitted and are operated by the driver. Tecalemit high pressure greasing system is fitted throughout, and a gear and hand-brake locking device is fitted to prevent passengers accidentally putting these into action.

The cost of the cars, for their seating accommodation of 46 passengers, is moderate, and it is the first case of this method of working, with two sets of engines being used, with English built chassis although, of course, Ford sets have been running for the last seven years on several of the associated lines

dealt with through Lt.-Col.H.F.Stephens' office.'

On first impressions the appearance of this set was not unlike that of the Fords though the box-shaped bodies were a little longer and the side doors were set back by a whole window space from the front. The appearance of the

Good use is about to be made of the baggage trailer. Note the electric gong and absence of headlights. Photograph Lens of Sutton.

Early view of the Shefflex running beside Pagham Harbour. Photograph Lens of Sutton.

bodies was enhanced by lining out the side and front lower body panels. The main body colour is believed to have been dark brown though this seems to have faded rather quickly in the seaside air. The toplights above the windows were top-hung and hinged outwards - it is not clear how such an arrangement could have avoided draughts as claimed in the *Locomotive Magazine* article. Spoked wheels were fitted and either lasted the entire life of the set or were replaced by identical wheels. Headlights were attached on independent mountings between the bonnet and the mudguards. A small rear light was fitted beneath the leading end of the left-hand running board

Shefflex looking the worse for wear at Selsey Town, with a bent mudguard and one of the headlights distinctly inoperable. Photograph Lens of Sutton.

36

Compare the draw gear and sturdy wheels on the Shefflex units to those fitted to the various Fords.

on the Chichester-facing car and under the right-hand running board on the Selsey-facing car. Sturdy buffer bars were fitted level with the bottom of the radiators which must have rather impeded access to the starting handles. Square-headed slotted drop pin couplers were fitted at the centre of the buffer bar with small coupling hooks on either side.

In service the Shefflex set proved rather noisier than the Fords and was inclined to slide out of control if the brakes were not applied with care. It has been claimed that sand boxes were fitted to remedy this but there is no obvious sign of such attachments in any of the photographs of this set. On the positive side the Shefflex axles and wheels are said to have been much more durable than those fitted to the Fords.

As road traffic increased so did the danger of collisions on the Tramway's ungated level crossings. A particularly concealed crossing existed at Stocksbridge Road and was the scene of a number of collisions. One of these was between the Shefflex set and a Southdown bus and resulted in a fractured crankshaft. Shefflex sent one of their fitters down to deal with this and the work is said to have taken six weeks to complete. A later collision with a lorry at the same crossing in 1932 left the set still coupled together but facing the line at almost 90degrees. Obviously the

exhaust-operated whistles were insufficiently audible and the set was fitted with electrically operated gongs in 1933 to signal their approach.

By 1934 the entire Selsey service was being operated by the Shefflex and Ford sets apart from one daily mixed train. Services were hopelessly uneconomic by this date and the line was closed on 19th January 1935. The Shefflex set was not included in the sale of the Tramway's assets but appears to have been sold separately by Stephens' executors at the same time as the rest of the rolling stock. The bodies were lifted from

the running gear and presumably saw further service as summer houses or garden sheds in the locality.

THE KENT & EAST SUSSEX SHEFFLEX RAILMOTOR SET

On the 5th December 1928 the K & E.S.R. Directors instructed Stephens to find out the cost of a new railcar and on the 22nd October 1929 their Minutes recorded that Stephens had purchased a railcar with £750 of his own money which was to be repaid to him by the issue of £938 in K & E.S.R. debentures. There is no record of this

Shefflex skirts Pagham Harbour during the growing season.

KES Shefflex stands in Rolvenden goods yard in the 1930s. The cylindrical object on the footboard appears to be a petrol tank but this was not the regular location for this item. Photograph National Railway Museum.

railmotor set in the Shefflex Motors order book but *Locomotive Magazine* covered its arrival in an article on 14th June 1930 as follows :

'SHEFFLEX RAIL CARS, KENT & EAST SUSSEX RY.

So satisfactory and economical in service have been the petrol railcars introduced by Lieut.-Col.H.F.Stephens on the West Sussex Ry. that he has recently acquired a similar set built by the Shefflex Motors Ltd of Tinsley, Sheffield, with certain modifications in the design, for the Kent & East Sussex Ry. (Headcorn to Robertsbridge).

The alterations made cover the new regulations of the Ministry of Transport, in addition to allowing a larger body to be used on the same chassis. This is made possible by halving the original bonnet and moving the dash board forward 18 in.; the driver's controls are carried forward by the same amount, but this does not in any way interfere with repairs, as the engine is quite accessible as before. Front-wheel brakes are now employed and these are of the screw type, and operate on the tyres. The petrol tank is fitted outside the body, and the engine feed is by the 'autovac' system.

Coming now to the accessories, 12 volt C.A.V. lighting sets are fitted, an electric

horn, explosion whistle and sanding gear are also provided and screen wipers are fitted. During the winter months the bodies are heated by the exhaust gases, but the hot-air pipes can easily be disconnected and thrown out of use in warm weather. The seating capacity of each coach is twenty-five, exclusive of driver; a total of fifty passengers can be carried, as the vehicles run back to back as illustrated; the wheelbase of

each is 11 ft. Half of the windows in the coaches are fixed and half are of the drop type. Of course all the controls are so arranged that they can be locked when the driver changes ends. A speed of 30 to 35 m.p.h. can be obtained.

Each car is fitted with a four-cylinder engine of 3 15/16 in. bore by 4 23/32 in. stroke, giving 24.8 h.p. at 1,200 revs per minute, or 47 h.p. at 1,600 revs. The bodies for this set were again built

Shefflex at Rolvenden platform. Note the air mechanism for the klaxon.

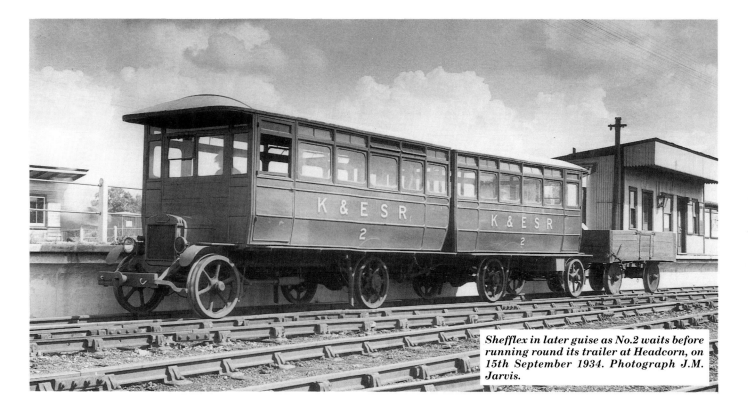

Shefflex in later guise as No.2 waits before running round its trailer at Headcorn, on 15th September 1934. Photograph J.M. Jarvis.

Early view of Shefflex at Robertsbridge, before fitting the roof headlamp. Photograph Lens of Sutton.

tion to the drop windows there were also opening toplights which could swivel diagonally for increased ventilation.

Pairs of headlights were fitted as on the Selsey railmotor set but the buffing gear was quite different. This consisted of a sturdy bar slightly wider than the bonnet and fitted slightly above axle level. A round slotted drop-pin coupling was fitted centrally with coupling hooks on either side. Curious curved brackets extended back from the ends of the buffer bars and ended in what appear to be light screw jacks positioned just in front of the wheels. These originally seem to have been fitted with grooved feet for fitting over the rails to provide support when lifting the cars but in later photos these 'feet' are missing and the threaded uprights do not appear long enough to have reached rail level, let

by Flear and are believed to have been originally intended for Stafford buses. The spoked flanged wheels were supplied by Wagon Repairs Ltd but rubber tyres were fitted to the rear wheels of each car in order for them to be towed through the streets to the nearest railhead where they were placed on low-loader wagons.

The body style was quite different from the earlier railmotors with a domed roof projecting beyond the body front and no luggage rails. The body sides were not lined but generously panelled with beading. The waist panels appear to have been fitted with two pairs of destination board brackets but there is no evidence that any attempt was ever made to use these. In addi-

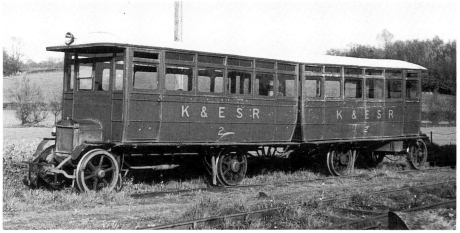

Shefflex at Rolvenden in 1935. Note clear view of sanding pipes. Photograph Rail Archive Stephenson.

Shefflex showing earlier style of painting and odd fittings in front of wheels. Photograph R.C. Riley Collection.

alone lift the cars. Perhaps additional parts were carried on board the set. Pipes for the sandboxes were fitted in front of the rear wheels and the petrol tanks appear to have been square fittings beneath the right-hand footboard on each car.

The cars are believed to have been delivered painted dark brown with K & E S R in shaded letters on the centre body panel and 3 on the lower bodyside, also in shaded lettering. The colour of the lettering does not seem to have been recorded but gives the impression of yel-low or gold shaded in red. The roof colour always seems to have been white. It is possible that single Shefflex and Ford cars could have been coupled together to form a hybrid set as is known to have happened on the Selsey Tramway but there is no evidence of this on

Shefflex in the rain at Rolvenden, with a good view of the extensive carriage stock partly displaced by the railmotors.

the K & E S R. It would certainly have made a bizarre sight if it ever happened.

This set seems to have performed as adequately as any of the others but passenger traffic fell steadily in the 1930s. As the railmotors could not be used on the mixed passenger and freight services it was inevitable that any cuts in services would fall more heavily on the railmotors than on the locomotive-hauled turns.

Minor changes took place in the appearance of these railmotors over the years. The pairs of headlights were replaced by single roof-mounted lights and the buffer bars were eventually removed. The square petrol tanks below the running boards gave way to cylindrical tanks mounted above the running boards and by 1935 the cars had been repainted with large white or yellow letters along each side reading K & E S R with a large 2 painted below the E. This presumably reflected the disposal of the first Ford set but does not explain why it was never felt necessary to number either of the Ford sets in any visible way.

The Shefflex set began to run intermittently after January 1938 and made its last run on 8th March 1938. It was then tucked away in the Rolvenden sidings with the second Ford set. On 8th August 1939 the two Shefflex bodies were sold with the surviving Ford body to Mr Smith for £2-15s-0d and the running gear is presumed to have been subsequently sold for scrap.

Above : Shefflex takes cover under the Rolvenden paint shop lean-to. Photo allegedly 1935 but headlamps indicate an earlier date. Photograph L&GRP.

Below : Shefflex waits in the loop outside Robertsbridge station. Note the excellent ventilation from the fully opening windows and the original paint scheme. Photograph L&GRP.

BAGGAGE TRAILERS

The Shropshire & Montgomeryshire trailer was rarely photographed in use with that line's Ford set which it clearly outlived, judging by this post-war view at Kinnerley. Shackles and chains in use, as well as the standard coupling.

Each of the lines which operated railmotors also acquired a light four-wheeled open wagon to run with them. These are generally referred to as baggage trailers although they served a variety of purposes.

WESTON CLEVEDON & PORTISHEAD RAILWAY

With the introduction of the first Drewry railmotor on this line it became apparent that the addition of a trailer would enable the railmotor to handle the extensive milk churn traffic. The Railway had some small wagons in stock and one of these, No.19, was adapted for use with the railmotor. No.19 was a 7 ft wheelbase three-plank drop-side wagon purchased from the Midland Railway and required little alteration to run with the railmotor since this was equipped with conventional drawgear at normal height. However, two stanchions were attached to each side so that dropping the sides would fill the gap between loading dock and wagon and enable churns to be manhandled onto the wagon with less risk of upset to the churn or physical injury to the train crew.

Despite No.19's small size it seems likely that it proved too heavy for the small Drewry and a special wagon was ordered from Cranes of Dereham to run with the railmotor instead. This was delivered on 21st September 1925. It had a capacity of 3 tons 10 cwt and was fitted with a three plank body measuring 12 ft x 7 ft with sides 18 inches high. There were hinged doors in the centre of each side but these seem to be missing in most photographs. The axles and their disc wheels were attached to the body's oak frame by a sort of cantilevered steel subframe. The wagon is believed to have been fitted with a handbrake but it is not clear what form this took as there is no brakegear evident in photographs. Buffer beams were fitted at normal height and were fitted with conventional hooks with screw couplings and cylindrical buffer blocks. The wagon does not appear to have been used when the

railmotor was hauling its passenger trailer and would not have been needed by the larger railmotor as this had a large goods compartment of its own. It seems to have been useful for general departmental work about the line and is coupled up to the Railway's Fordson rail tractor in some photographs. It was presumably sent off to Swindon with the rest of the rolling stock when the line closed.

SHROPSHIRE AND MONTGOMERYSHIRE RAILWAY

Apart from one publicity photograph of the Ford railmotor set shortly after delivery there is little photographic evidence relating to the use of this line's baggage trailer. This trailer is believed to have been acquired with the railmotor set in 1923 but to have been built by Cranes rather than Edmonds. It had a three plank body with a central bottom-hinged door in each side and vertical external strapping midway between the door and each end and on either side

The Selsey trailer in November 1928, in its low-sided condition. Compare with the original condition shown on page 28. Photograph H.C. Casserley.

of the coupling at each end. Its running gear seems to have been similar to that fitted to the W & C.P.R. trailer but was set much lower to the ground to match the lower bodyline of the Ford set.

Since the Ford set was never fitted with couplings at its outer ends the trailer had to be coupled between the cars and was fitted with slotted square drop pin centre couplings for this purpose and very basic buffing blocks at each corner. Coupled in this way the trailer would have made access between the cars difficult and this may explain its apparently infrequent use on the line. It appears in a number of photographs of the dump siding at Kinnerley in the 1930s but its subsequent fate is not known.

SELSEY TRAMWAY
The trailer supplied to this line also seems to have come with its Ford set and in later years bore a striking resemblance to the S & M.R. trailer. As delivered the Selsey trailer was a five-plank vehicle with internal vertical strapping. It had a central bottom-hinged door and running gear and disc wheels similar to the other Cranes vehicles. When running with the Ford set it had to run between the cars as these had no outer couplings.

By the time that the Shefflex set had been delivered in 1928 the trailer was a three plank vehicle with external strapping and centre coupling arrangements exactly as fitted to the S & M.R. trailer. The only difference between the Selsey trailer and the Shropshire trailer is the absence of buffing blocks from

the Selsey example. There is an outside possibility that some accident befell the Selsey trailer and that it was replaced by the loan of the Shropshire trailer but the absence of buffing blocks makes this unlikely. The original height of the trailer may simply have made access between the two cars of the Ford set too difficult and it was cut down to a more convenient size.

As the Shefflex cars had outer couplings it was possible to attach the trailer to either end of this set but it was frequently coupled between the cars as this removed any need for shunting between trips. The Selsey

trailer was extremely well used for almost every class of traffic, ranging from prams and ice cream carts to small livestock and the more adventurous class of passenger in fine weather.

At the closure of the line the trailer was lined up at Chichester with the property belonging to Stephens' executors, the Shefflex set and the locomotive MOROUS. It is not clear how these were disposed of but it is probable that they went for scrap separately from the rest of the line's stock.

KENT & EAST SUSSEX RAILWAY
This line did not acquire its trailer until the arrival of its Shefflex set in 1929. This is believed to have been another Cranes vehicle, certainly the K & E.S.R. purchased spares from Cranes in the years that followed the trailer's arrival. It was a five-plank vehicle with internal strapping and central bottom-hinged doors to each side. It was similar to the Selsey trailer in its original state but differed significantly in possessing a very visible hand brake at one end.

Photographs only show this trailer running with the Shefflex set. However, the second Ford set was fitted with coupling gear at about the time that the trailer arrived and it would have been possible for the trailer to have run with this set too. This trailer always seems to have been attached behind the railmotor set rather than between the cars.

This trailer was adopted by the permanent way staff after the disposal of the railmotors and seems to have survived in departmental use until Nationalisation. Its subsequent fate has gone unrecorded but it is likely to have been one of the many vehicles burnt at Headcorn in 1948.

KESR trailer off the tracks at Rolvenden. Note the prominent brake lever and coupling gear.

CONCLUSION

In the absence of authoritative data any assessment of the railmotors must to an extent be speculative. It has been alleged that their noise, smell and jolting motion deterred passengers from travelling on the lines which used them but there are plenty of photographs showing them with healthy loadings of apparently happy passengers. Such passengers would not have had to put up with the long delays suffered on the mixed locomotive-hauled trains which paused at every station to add and detach vans and wagons and whose own motion was far from smooth on the increasingly decrepit rails of the Stephens railways between the Wars.

Given the increasing pressures on rural railways during the railmotors' period of operations it seems that they played a crucial part in keeping their lines going. If the main line companies had shown more interest in the possibilities of the internal combustion railmotor it is perfectly feasible that a further generation of railmotors would have been acquired second-hand as happened in the United States and France. In the absence of anything remotely affordable, and in the absence of Stephens' own private purse, it is not surprising that the few Stephens' railways to survive the mid-thirties reverted to locomotive haulage. The Drewry car purchased from the Southern for the WC&PLR shows what might have happened if more such vehicles had been available.

Whilst speculating may we be forgiven for considering some far-fetched possibilities that did not take place? Stephens may have attached a horse tram behind GAZELLE but he never seems to have considered the American practice of purchasing electric streetcars and converting them to petrol operation. He also seems to have been unaware of the example of the Salzkammergutlokalbahn in Austria which converted its own royal saloon into a railmotor by filling its baggage compartment with '...a very small petrol engine and a very big electric power plant.' Whilst neither of Stephens' royal saloons would have justified such a conversion it is possible to contemplate a similar project having been undertaken with the Kent & East Sussex steam railmotor, to give it a further lease of life.

It must not be forgotten that Stephens even considered the possibility of electric operation. The East Kent Railway contemplated it from the start and the abortive Southern Heights Light Railway would have been operated by standard Southern Railway third rail electric stock, if it had been built. Above all there was Stephens' own patent for electric booster motors to be fitted to the tenders of steam locomotives to assist them up steep gradients; again the source of power would have been an electrified third rail.

Colonel Stephens' railmotors are remembered as quaint and eccentric. In a slow news week they would even get a mention in the national press under such headlines as THIS BUS RUNS ON THE WRONG LINES. It must be remembered that the contemporary railway press, albeit a fairly uncritical one, made no such jokes and treated them as a serious solution to the problem of rural branch lines. They had their faults but the final verdict must be that they did the job they were intended to do - more or less.

BIBLIOGRAPHY

Periodic Publications: THE LOCOMOTIVE MAGAZINE April & September 1923, February 1928, June 1930. RAILWAY GAZETTE November 1924. THE RAILWAY YEAR BOOK. THE UNIVERSAL DIRECTORY OF RAILWAY OFFICIALS. BRADSHAW'S RAILWAY GUIDE. THE TENTERDEN TERRIER, Journal of the Tenterden Railway Company. THE COLONEL, Journal of the Colonel Stephens Society.
Histories: BRITISH STANDARD GAUGE LIGHT RAILWAYS by R W Kidner, Oakwood Press. MULTIPLE UNIT TRAINS, RAILMOTORS & TRAMCARS 1829-1947 by R W Kidner, Oakwood Press. BRITISH STEAM RAILCARS by R W Rush, Oakwood Press. THE COLONEL STEPHENS RAILWAYS by John Scott-Morgan, David & Charles. THE WESTON CLEVEDON & PORTISHEAD RAILWAY by Christopher Redwood, Sequoia Publishing. THE WESTON CLEVEDON & PORTISHEAD RAILWAY by Peter Strange, Twelveheads Press. THE WESTON CLEVEDON & PORTISHEAD LIGHT RAILWAY by Colin Maggs, Oakwood Press. THE ROTHER VALLEY RAILWAY, LATER THE KENT & EAST SUSSEX RAILWAY by Maurice Lawson Finch. THE KENT & EAST SUSSEX RAILWAY by Stephen Garrett, Oakwood Press. BRANCHLINE TO TENTERDEN by V Mitchell & K Smith, Middleton Press. THE SHROPSHIRE & MONTGOMERYSHIRE RAILWAY by Eric Tonks, Industrial Railway Society. BRANCHLINE TO SHREWSBURY by V Mitchell & K Smith, Middleton Press. THE SHROPSHIRE & MONTGOMERYSHIRE RAILWAY by Keith & Susan Turner, David & Charles. THE CRIGGION BRANCH by Roger Carpenter, Wild Swan Press. THE HUNDRED OF MANHOOD & SELSEY TRAMWAYS by E.C.Griffith. BRANCH LINE TO SELSEY by V Mitchell & K Smith, Middleton Press. THE NORTH EAST RAILWAY BOOK by Ken Hoole, David & Charles. THE COUNTY DONEGAL RAILWAYS by Edward M Patterson, David & Charles. THE FESTINIOG RAILWAY by J I C Boyd, Oakwood Press. THE RYE & CAMBER TRAMWAY by Peter A Harding. THE SHEPPEY LIGHT RAILWAY by Peter A Harding.
Documents at the Public Record Office: RAIL 332/1-3 Minute Books of the Kent & East Sussex Railway. MT6 1887/5 Application to install siding at Bodiam Station. RAIL 621/1 Minute Book of the Shropshire & Montgomeryshire Railway.
We would also like to acknowledge the assistance of John Miller and Philip Shaw of the Colonel Stephens Railway Museum & Archives for permission to consult documents in their care. Similarly we are very grateful for the assistance of the Festiniog Railway Society and the Curator and staff of the Public Record Office, Kew.